Summary of

The Point of it All
Charles Krauthammer

Conversation Starters

By Paul Adams
Book Habits

Please Note: This is an unofficial Conversation Starters guide. If you have not yet read the original work, you can purchase the original book here.

Copyright © 2018 by BookHabits. All Rights Reserved. First Published in the United States of America 2018

We hope you enjoy this complimentary guide from BookHabits. Our mission is to aid readers and reading groups with quality thought-provoking material to in the discovery and discussions on some of today's favorite books.

Disclaimer / Terms of Use: This guide is unofficial and unauthorized. It is not authorized, approved, licensed, or endorsed by the original book's author or publisher and any of their licensees or affiliates. Product names, logos, brands, and other trademarks featured or referred to within this publication are the property of their respective trademark holders and are not affiliated with BookHabits. The publisher and author make no representations or warranties with respect to the accuracy or completeness of these contents and disclaim all warranties such as warranties of fitness for a particular purpose.

No part of this publication may be reproduced or retransmitted, electronic or mechanical, without the written permission of the publisher.

Bonus Downloads
*Get Free Books with **Any Purchase** of Conversation Starters!*

Every purchase comes with a FREE download!

Add spice to any conversation
Never run out of things to say
Spend time with those you love

Get It Now

or Click Here.

Scan Your Phone

Tips for Using Conversation Starters:

EVERY GOOD BOOK CONTAINS A WORLD FAR DEEPER THAN the surface of its pages. Questions herein are designed to bring us beneath the surface of the page and invite us into the world that lives on. These questions can be used to:

- Foster a deeper understanding of the book
- Promote an atmosphere of discussion for groups
- Assist in the study of the book, either individually or corporately
- Explore unseen realms of the book as never seen before

Table of Contents

Introducing *The Point of it All* 6

Discussion Questions 16

Introducing the Author 37

Fireside Questions 45

Quiz Questions 56

Quiz Answers 69

Ways to Continue Your Reading 70

Introducing *The Point of it All*

The Point of it All: A Lifetime of Great Loves and Endeavors* is a book written by political commentator Charles Krauthammer. It is a collection of his writings as a columnist for various publications tackling a wide range of issues including the philosophical, political and the personal. It includes unpublished speeches and an essay of populist politics and its effect on democracy around the world. It is considered the most intimate of the books Krauthammer has written and is edited by his son Daniel Krauthammer.

The author is a known for his opinion columns the writing of which, critics say, have reached the level of art. His unique insights and wit have found expression through his writings which tackle foreign policy, statecraft, medical ethics, spaceflight, and even baseball. Krauthammer worked on the collection before he died in June 2018 and featured speeches, columns, and unpublished works that serve as proof of his original ideas and wise words on the state of American history, politics, and democratic pursuits. It also features his personal views on issues that are personally important to him including family, friendship, and values he observed while still alive. His works demonstrate intellectual sharpness, integrity, and clarity, making him an outstanding thinker of his generation. The essays show the real person behind his words. This book is a testament to his belief in using a critical and honest mind to understand the urgent issues of the day.

Though known for his regular appearance on Fox News where he discussed current events with his trademark combination of calm, logic and intellect, Krauthammer is primarily a writer who wrote columns for *Time, The Washington Post*, the *Weekly Standard*, and *The New Republic*. His last column was written on June 8, 2018, for *The Washington Post*. He wrote that he had few weeks to live and is sad about it, "but I leave with the knowledge that I lived the life I intended." The book is divided into five parts with 18 chapters in all. Part 1 is entitled "What A Piece of Work Man Is." The four other parts of the book are respectively Man and Society; Politics, Foreign and Domestic; Competing Visions, and Speaking in the First Person. The chapters in Part One include Life Well-Lived, Customs, and Culture, Contests, The Doctor Is In, and Matters of Life and Death. Chapter One includes his thoughts as a "Newborn Father," and his profiles of political personalities like Ronald Reagan, Thomas Jefferson, Pope John Paul II, as well as cultural icons like Isiah Berlin and Irving Kristol. He dedicated the book to his wife Robyn, who has "co-authored" his life, and to his son Daniel whose "brilliant mind has been an incredible influence…".

On Ronald Reagan, he wrote in a 2004 article for *Time* that the man had courage and conviction and that he used these two qualities to win the Cold War. Time has shown that the shallow explanations about Reagan's success have not endured but his "largeness and deeply enduring significance" remains. He also praised Pope John Paul II who, during his time in the 80s, used the power of faith to mobilize Christians. He saw the Pope as one who "sparked, tended and fanned the flames of freedom in Poland" and the rest of Eastern Europe. Reagan, Pope John Paul II, Winston Churchill, and Franklin Delano Roosevelt are "the great liberators of the 20th century," according to Krauthammer. President George W. Bush, he said, is cited for his attempts to liberate and establish democracy in Afghanistan and other Middle East countries but this attempt failed because Afghanistan is too primitive and too fractured. He thinks Bush will be remembered for keeping Americans safe after 9/11 for creating an anti-terrorism infrastructure. He compared Bush to Harry Truman whose legacy was not immediately appreciated, but as time passed, history slowly saw him favorably. Bush's legacy will be appreciated later on in history, Krauthammer thought. Barrack Obama, on the other hand, has not performed well according to Krauthammer. The American success in the Iraq war was not sustained by the Obama administration. The Russian influence has become a paramount in Europe because of Obama's liberal worldview. Krauthammer disapproved Obama's statement that "no one nation can and should try to dominate another nation." Neither did the author think well of Donald Trump though he also criticized the Trump Derangement Syndrome exhibited by the left. He disapproved of Trump's "America First" slogan and said he committed a big mistake in turning away from free trade. Trump has likewise made an unwise move in undermining NATO and US joint programs and for encouraging authoritarian leaders around the globe. In writing about social issues, Krauthammer was ambivalent about the conservative stance. He didn't think Roe vs. Wade was a good decision, explaining that late-term abortions were not right, but women still deserve to have abortion rights. He supported the idea of the sanctity of marriage but also approved gay marriage. Scientific explanations of climate change are not yet conclusive, he said but encouraged American industries to burn fewer fossil fuels. Krauthammer had many more thoughts on mundane issues like sailing, chess, golf, baseball, fatherhood, medical practice, movies, and space travel. He also dedicated an article to his beloved wife Robyn.

His son, Daniel, writes the introduction and pays tribute to his father. He explains that his father intended to write a book on foreign policy, having started with an essay that is part of the book. In writing about the future, Krauthammer expressed his fears of the emergence of authoritarianism throughout the world, led by Russia and China. Authoritarianism in Western Europe and the United States has become apparent.

The New York Journal of Books review says Krauthammer "exhibits a very pessimistic worldview" in his belief of a "worldwide shift towards authoritarianism." The review says his pessimism is "almost Spenglerian." The review expresses hope that "Krauthammer's gifts of observation and analysis failed him." *National Review* says Krauthammer is a "giant" who "defended our civilization" and "represented what's best in it." The *Washington Post* says the author provoked readers to think, expanded readers' understanding, and made them laugh as well. His column has a "breathtaking range and intelligence and integrity." Condoleezza Rice says the author is "voice of reason" whose powerful intelligence served the cause of Democracy.

The Point of it All is a *New York Times* bestseller. It is written by the same author of the #1 the *New York Times* bestseller *Things That Matter*.

Discussion Questions

"Get Ready to Enter a New World"

Tip: Begin with questions dealing with broader issues to ensure ample time for quality discussions. Read through all discussion questions before engaging.

question 1

The author is a known for his opinion columns, the writing of which, critics say, have reached the level of art. His unique insights and wit have found expression through his writings which tackle foreign policy, statecraft, medical ethics, spaceflight, and even baseball. In what way are his writings considered art? What is artistic about them?

~ ~ ~

question 2

Krauthammer worked on the collection before he died in June 2018 and featured speeches, columns, and unpublished works that serve as proof of his original ideas and wise words on the state of American history, politics, and democratic pursuits. It also features his personal views on issues that are personally important to him including family, friendship, and values he observed while still alive. Why do you think he put the personal writings along with his political and social views? Could he have separated the personal from the rest?

~ ~ ~

~~~

question 3

His works demonstrate intellectual sharpness, integrity, and clarity, making him an outstanding thinker of his generation. Who are the other political commentators of his generation? How do they compare to him?

~~~

~~~

question 4

Though known for his regular appearance on Fox News where he discussed current events with his trademark combination of calm, logic and intellect, Krauthammer is primarily a writer who wrote columns for Time, The Washington Post, the Weekly Standard, and The New Republic. Have you read his columns? Which particular essay do you remember him for? Why?

~~~

~~~

question 5

His last column was written on June 8, 2018, for The Washington Post. He wrote that he had few weeks to live and is sad about it, "but I leave with the knowledge that I lived the life I intended." How do you feel about his announcement of his impending death?

~~~

~~~

question 6

The book is divided into five parts with 18 chapters in all. Part 1 is entitled "What A Piece of Work Man Is" and has the chapters Life Well-Lived, Customs and Culture, Contests, The Doctor Is In, and Matters of Life and Death. Why does the title Part 1 "What A Piece of Work Man Is? How do the chapters relate to Part One's title?

~~~

~~~

question 7

Chapter One includes his thoughts as a "Newborn Father," and his profiles of political personalities like Ronald Reagan, Thomas Jefferson, Pope John Paul II, as well as cultural icons like Isiah Berlin and Irving Kristol. Why do you think he put these subjects in the first chapter?

~~~

~~~

question 8

He dedicated the book to his wife Robyn, who has "co-authored" his life, and to his son Daniel whose "brilliant mind has been an incredible influence...". What does this say of him as a person?

~~~

~~~

question 9

On Ronald Reagan, he wrote in a 2004 article for Time that the man had courage and conviction and that he used these two qualities to win the Cold War. Time has shown that the shallow explanations about Reagan's success have not endured but his "largeness and deeply enduring significance" remains. Do you agree with him? Why? Why not?

~~~

~~~

question 10

He also praised Pope John Paul II who, during his time in the 80s, used the power of faith to mobilize Christians. He saw the Pope as one who "sparked, tended and fanned the flames of freedom in Poland" and the rest of Eastern Europe. Does this change your view of the Pope? How did you think of him before reading the author's views about the Pope?

~~~

question 11

He disapproved of Trump's "America First" slogan and said he committed a big mistake in turning away from free trade. Trump has likewise made an unwise move in undermining NATO and US joint programs and for encouraging authoritarian leaders around the globe. Why did he disapprove of the slogan "America First"?

~~~

question 12

He compared George W. Bush to Harry Truman whose legacy was not immediately appreciated, but as time passed, history slowly saw him favorably. Bush's legacy will be appreciated later on in history, Krauthammer thought. What did he think is Bush's legacy?

~~~

~~~

question 13

The American success in the Iraq war was not sustained by the Obama administration. The Russian influence has become a paramount in Europe because of Obama's liberal worldview. Krauthammer disapproved of Obama's statement that "no one nation can and should try to dominate another nation." Do you agree with him about Obama? Why? Why not?

~~~

question 14

In writing about the future, Krauthammer expressed his fears of the emergence of authoritarianism throughout the world, led by Russia and China. Authoritarianism in Western Europe and the United States is also becoming apparent. How do you feel about his expressed fear?

~~~

question 15

Krauthammer had many more thoughts on mundane issues like sailing, chess, golf, baseball, fatherhood, medical practice, movies, and space travel. He also dedicated an article to his beloved wife. What kind of person was he based on his writings about the non-political?

~~~

~~~

question 16

The Point of it All is a New York Times bestseller. Krauthammer also wrote the #1 the New York Times bestseller Things That Matter. Why do you think his books are bestsellers?

~~~

question 17

The New York Journal of Books review says Krauthammer "exhibits a very pessimistic worldview" in his belief of a "worldwide shift towards authoritarianism." The review says his pessimism is "almost Spenglerian." The review expresses hope that "Krauthammer's gifts of observation and analysis failed him." Do you think he is too pessimistic? What is his basis for being pessimistic about the future?

~~~

question 18

National Review says Krauthammer is a "giant" who "defended our civilization" and "represented what's best in it." What does the review mean by calling him a giant?

~~~

question 19

The Washington Post says the author provoked readers to think, expanded readers' understanding, and made them laugh as well. His column has a "breathtaking range and intelligence and integrity." What is included in this breathtaking range? How does he expand your understanding?

~~~

~ ~ ~

question 20

Condoleezza Rice says the author is a "voice of reason" whose powerful intelligence served the cause of Democracy. Why does Krauthammer think Democracy is worth advocating for?

~ ~ ~

Introducing the Author

Charles Krauthammer was a commentator at Fox News' Special Report with Bret Baier, appearing on the news program every night. His syndicated column for *The Washington Post* was published by over 400 newspapers all over the globe. It was as a writer for the *Post* that he won the 1987 Pulitzer prize. He also authored another collection of columns, *Things That Matter: Three Decades of Passions, Pastimes and Politics* which became a #1 *New York Times* bestseller, selling over a million copies.

He studied medicine at Harvard University and served at the Massachusetts General Hospital, eventually becoming chief of the psychiatry department. It was during his time here that he co-discovered one form of bipolar ailment. In 1978, he joined the Carter administration as a member of the psychiatric research team. He soon became a speechwriter for Vice President Walter Mondale and a writer for *The New Republic.* His essays for the magazine won him the National Magazine Award for Essays and Criticism. He worked with the Council on Bioethics from 2001 to 2006.

Krauthammer was named by the *Financial Times* in 2006 as the "most influential commentator in America," citing his influence on American foreign policy for over two decades. He is cited by fellow columnists as the conservative voice who lead the right during the Obama years. He was a "powerful force in American conservatism." Former president Bill Clinton acknowledged him in 2010 as "a brilliant man," to which Krauthammer responded, "my career is done…I'm toast." He won the William F. Buckley Award for Media Excellence in 2013.

In his February 20, 2014 column, he wrote that "I'm not a global warming believer. I'm not a global warming denier." He explained that global warming science is not settled. He is known for his opposition to capital punishment and his criticism of the intelligent design movement. He wrote articles explaining how intelligent design is "tarted-up creationism" and called for a scientific consensus on evolution. He believed that the controversy pitting religion against science is a false conflict.

He co-founded the Pro Musica Hebraica with his wife Robyn, a nonprofit organization that aimed to recover Jewish classical music and have these performed in concert halls. The organization premiered Jewish compositions unearthed from archives from different parts of Europe, featuring world-renowned artists like Itzhak Perlman and Evgeny Kissin. He established the Krauthammer Fellowship, aimed to support writers, journalists, and editors to work with *Mosaic Magazine* and support works related to Jewish culture, American democracy, and the modern state of Israel. The Dr. Charles Krauthammer Memorial Scholarship was established by Fox News Channel to honor Krauthammer's legacy. Fox works with the National Merit Scholarship Program to benefit college-bound children of Fox employees. Krauthammer also supports the Shepherd Center, a hospital based in Atlanta, Georgia which specializes in the research and treatment of spinal cord and brain injuries. He was a member of the Council of Foreign Relations and the Chess Journalists of America.

Krauthammer was paralyzed from the waist down in a diving board accident, during his first year in medical school. He was in the hospital for 14 months. He continued studying medicine after the accident and graduated in 1975. He married his wife Robyn in 1974. She used to be a lawyer and stopped her legal practice in order to focus on creating art. They have one child, Daniel, who edited his father's last book. Of Jewish descent, he claimed he is not religious but likened himself to Shintoists who engage in ancestor worship. His religious beliefs were influenced by his philosophy professor Rabbi David Hartman who now heads the Shalom Hartman Institute in Jerusalem. Krauthammer had an operation in August 2017 that removed a tumor from his abdomen. Cancer returned after less than a year. At age 68, he died of cancer of the small intestine on June 21, 2018, in Atlanta, Georgia.

Bonus Downloads
*Get Free Books with **Any Purchase** of* Conversation Starters!

Every purchase comes with a FREE download!

Add spice to any conversation
Never run out of things to say
Spend time with those you love

Get it Now

or Click Here.

Scan Your Phone

Fireside Questions

"What would you do?"

Tip: These questions can be a fun exercise as it spurs creativity among the readers by allowing alternate scene endings and "if this was you" questions.

~~~

question 21

He studied medicine at Harvard University and served at the Massachusetts General Hospital, eventually becoming chief of the psychiatry department. It was during his time here that he co-discovered one form of bipolar ailment. In 1978, he joined the Carter administration. Why do you think he left his medical career for political writing?

~~~

question 22

Krauthammer was named by the Financial Times in 2006 as the "most influential commentator in America," citing his influence on American foreign policy for over two decades. He is cited by fellow columnists as the conservative voice who lead the right during the Obama years. He was a "powerful force in American conservatism." Former president Bill Clinton acknowledged him in 2010 as "a brilliant man," to which Krauthammer responded, "my career is made…I'm toast." What do you think did he mean with his response to Clinton? How is it related to his being a conservative?

~~~

question 23

He is known for his opposition to capital punishment and his criticism of the intelligent design movement. He wrote articles explaining how intelligent design is "tarted-up creationism" and called for a scientific consensus on evolution. He believed that the controversy pitting religion against science is a false conflict. Did you learn anything from him about science and religion? Do you agree with him? Why? Why not?

~~~

~~~

question 24

He co-founded the Pro Musica Hebraica with his wife Robyn, a nonprofit organization that aimed to recover Jewish classical music and have these performed in concert halls. The organization premiered Jewish compositions unearthed from archives from different parts of Europe, featuring world-renowned artists like Itzhak Perlman and Evgeny Kissin. What were his other philanthropic activities?

~~~

~~~

question 25

Krauthammer was paralyzed from the waist down in a diving board accident during his first year in medical school. He was in the hospital for 14 months. He continued studying medicine after the accident and graduated in 1975. He married his wife Robyn in 1974. How did he deal with his paralyzed condition?

~~~

question 26

He studied medicine at Harvard University and served at the Massachusetts General Hospital, eventually becoming chief of the psychiatry department. It was during his time here that he co-discovered one form of bipolar ailment. If he continued his medical career how successful would he be today?

~~~

question 27

Krauthammer was paralyzed from the waist down in a diving board accident, during his first year in medical school. He was in the hospital for 14 months. He continued studying medicine after the accident and graduated in 1975. He married his wife Robyn in 1974. If he did not have the accident, how would his life have been? What kind of person would he have turned out to be?

~~~

question 28

The book is divided into five parts with 18 chapters in all. Part 1 is entitled "What A Piece of Work Man Is." The four other parts of the book are respectively Man and Society; Politics, Foreign and Domestic; Competing Visions, and Speaking in the First Person. If you are to reorder the organization of the book to suit your favored themes, how would you do it?

question 29

Barrack Obama has not performed well according to Krauthammer. The American success in the Iraq war was not sustained by the Obama administration. The Russian influence has become a paramount in Europe because of Obama's liberal worldview. Krauthammer disapproved of Obama's statement that "no one nation can and should try to dominate another nation." If Obama listened to Krauthammer for advice, how would America be today?

question 30

Neither did the author think well of Donald Trump though he also criticized the Trump Derangement Syndrome exhibited by the left. He disapproved of Trump's "America First" slogan and said he committed a big mistake in turning away from free trade. Trump has likewise done an unwise move in undermining NATO and US joint programs and for encouraging authoritarian leaders around the globe. If Krauthammer ran for president and won, what would be his legacy?

Quiz Questions

"Ready to Announce the Winners?"

Tip: Create a leaderboard and track scores to see who gets the most correct answers. Winners required. Prizes optional.

~~~

quiz question 1

The book is divided into five parts with 18 chapters in all. Part 1 is entitled_____. The four other parts of the book are respectively Man and Society; Politics, Foreign and Domestic; Competing Visions, and Speaking in the First Person.

~~~

~~~

quiz question 2

He dedicated the book to _____, who has "co-authored" his life, and to his son Daniel whose "brilliant mind has been an incredible influence…".

~~~

quiz question 3

He wrote in a 2004 article for Time that _____ had courage and conviction and that he used these two qualities to win the Cold War. Time has shown that the shallow explanations about the former president's success have not endured but his "largeness and deeply enduring significance" remains.

~~~

~~~

quiz question 4

True or False: He praised Pope John Paul II who, during his time in the 80s, used the power of faith to mobilize Christians. He saw the Pope as one who "sparked, tended and fanned the flames of freedom in Poland" and the rest of Eastern Europe.

~~~

~~~

quiz question 5

True or False: Reagan, Pope John Paul II, Winston Churchill, and Franklin Delano Roosevelt are "the great liberators of the 20th century," according to Krauthammer.

~~~

~~~

quiz question 6

True or False: He thinks Trump will be remembered for keeping Americans safe after 9/11 for creating an anti-terrorism infrastructure. He compared him to Harry Truman whose legacy was not immediately appreciated, but as time passed, history slowly saw him favorably. Trump's legacy will be appreciated later on in history, Krauthammer thought.

~~~

~~~

quiz question 7

True or False: Barrack Obama, on the other hand, has not performed well according to Krauthammer. The American success in the Iraq war was not sustained by the Obama administration. The Russian influence has become a paramount in Europe because of Obama's liberal worldview. Krauthammer disapproved of Obama's statement that "no one nation can and should try to dominate another nation."

~~~

~~~

quiz question 8

He co-founded the _____ with his wife Robyn, a nonprofit organization that aimed to recover Jewish classical music and have these performed in concert halls. The organization premiered Jewish compositions unearthed from archives from different parts of Europe, featuring world-renowned artists like Itzhak Perlman and Evgeny Kissin.

~~~

~~~

quiz question 9

He established the Krauthammer Fellowship, aimed to support writers, journalists, and editors to work with _____ Magazine and support works related to Jewish culture, American democracy, and the modern state of Israel.

~~~

~~~

quiz question 10

True or False: The Dr. Charles Krauthammer Memorial Scholarship was established by Fox News Channel to honor Krauthammer's legacy. Fox works with the National Merit Scholarship Program to benefit college-bound children of Fox employees.

~~~

~~~

quiz question 11

True or False: Of Jewish descent, he claimed he is not religious but likened himself to Shintoists who engage in ancestor worship. His religious beliefs were influenced by his philosophy professor Rabbi David Hartman who now heads the Shalom Hartman Institute in Jerusalem.

~~~

~~~

quiz question 12

True or False: He wrote articles explaining how intelligent design is "tarted-up creationism" and called for a scientific consensus on evolution. He believed that the controversy pitting religion against science is a false conflict.

~~~

Quiz Answers

1. "What A Piece of Work Man Is"
2. his wife, Robyn
3. Ronald Reagan
4. True
5. True
6. False
7. True
8. Pro Musica Hebraica
9. Mosaic
10. True
11. True
12. True

Ways to Continue Your Reading

Every month, our team runs through a wide selection of books to pick the best titles for readers and reading groups, and promotes these titles to our thousands of readers – sometimes with free downloads, sale dates, and additional brochures.

[Click here to sign up for these benefits.](#)

If you have not yet read the original work or would like to read it again, you can purchase the original book here.

Bonus Downloads
*Get Free Books with **Any Purchase** of Conversation Starters!*

Every purchase comes with a FREE download!

Add spice to any conversation
Never run out of things to say
Spend time with those you love

Get it Now

or Click Here.

Scan Your Phone

On the Next Page…

If you found this book helpful to your discussions and rate it a 4 or 5, please write us a review on the next page.

Any length would be fine but we'd appreciate hearing you more! We'd be very encouraged.

Till next time,

BookHabits

"Loving Books is Actually a Habit"